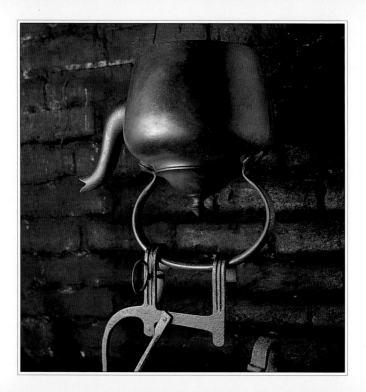

Cottage Interiors

Cottage Interiors

Photographs by Peter Rauter

WEIDENFELD

COUNTRY
MINIATURES

WEIDENFELD AND NICOLSON

LONDON

INTRODUCTION

*W*HETHER the unassuming house of a working farm, a stone croft nestling in rugged hills, or a black-and-white house set neatly into a small village, the English cottage to many represents all that is best about life in the country. As various as the cottages themselves are the people who live in them, and the uses to which they are put: some cottages are truly lived and worked in, simple as they are, while others serve as idyllic retreats far from the bustle of city life.

Looking back at the development of the cottage, we see that like the people who lived in them, they have changed with the sands of

time. Emerging from the Middle Ages, the cottage in the sixteenth century was little more than a couple of ground-floor rooms with modest sleeping quarters above. The seventeenth century brought more sophistication, a room or two more and greater refinement of many of the internal features. Symmetry and grandeur took precedence in the eighteenth century.

The cottage is above all a very personal place, a private hideaway where objects of affection are squirreled away, where family heirlooms are accumulated and where memories are created, remembered and forgotten. What is contained in these cottages reflects not so much the conscious taste of their owners as their history, their way of thinking, their passions and odd habits – perhaps this is exactly why the English cottage is so marvellously quirky.

For that very reason, however, the interiors of most cottages are not seen by many. Apart from immediate family, close friends or relatives, few are fortunate enough to gain entry. But once inside, a world opens up, and it is this realm that this book enters, in a celebration of all the idiosyncracies these wonderful cottages embody.

WILTSHIRE

*T*N this seventeenth-century cottage, the fireplace, which forms the centrepiece of the low-ceilinged room, features several of the classical motifs that were popular in early English Renaissance buildings. The original fireplace opening has been surrounded with a guilloche moulding of interlacing circles.

BUCKINGHAMSHIRE

*O*NE almost has the feeling that this tiny living room was built within the roots of a great old tree. The subterranean sensation is enhanced by the unhewn beams, leaning clay wall and a plaster ceiling that is held together with twigs.

SUFFOLK

W ITHIN the timber-framing of a restored
seventeenth-century former inn is a late-
eighteenth-century eastern German painted
cupboard that stands out beautifully against the
frescolike red paint, whose erosion has given it
a subtle patina.

WILTSHIRE

*T*HE elegance of the seventeenth-century oak panelling in this living room is embellished with a marquetry chest-on-stand of the same period, while the cruder, wide timber of the floors heightens the interplay of woods.

HEREFORD AND
WORCESTER

*P*ERHAPS nothing evokes cottage life more than the presence of farm animals. Many working kitchens of the past are used today for other activities, but that hasn't stopped these hens from feeding on the table.

WEST SUSSEX

*F*ORMERLY a bakehouse, this room is as useful as it was during its former incarnation; it is used today as a store room. The uneven brick floor is commonly found in Sussex, and the yellow door is characteristic of the area.

Cumbria

$\mathscr{D}$OVE Cottage at Grasmere was home to William Wordsworth between 1799 and 1808. A classic mid-nineteenth-century range, a model typical of the North Country, is the focal point of a kitchen that has a lead-lined timber sink and only a small window placed high up.

DURHAM

*I*N the wash house of a seventeenth-century farmhouse, which has been restored and authenticated with period objects, are a number of time-worn but still useful objects, like the washerboard and large stone sink.

OXFORDSHIRE

*I*N this small bedroom, tucked within the steeply sloping ceiling of an eighteenth-century cottage near Chipping Norton, a canopy effect has been created over the brass bed with striped cotton ticking swagged over a pole and trimmed with tassels. The doors, too, conform to the roofline.

———❖———

SURREY

*F*ROM its beginning as an early-sixteenth-century cottage, this little building has grown to include an eighteenth-century addition. The medieval origins of the house can be detected in its back wall, into which a magnificent fireplace has been placed.

HEREFORD AND WORCESTER

*T*HE blackness of this kitchen belies its lived-in character. The lives of past generations can be perceived in the well-worn sandstone floor and a hearth that has changed shape to accommodate the technological advances reflected in the Victorian range.

WEST SUSSEX

*B*EGUILING patterns have resulted from the conversion of a sixteenth-century water tower for residential use. The timberwork was inserted within the tower, creating an unusual visual effect that is difficult to place in an architectural tradition.

HEREFORD AND WORCESTER

*T*HE blackness of this kitchen belies its lived-in character. The lives of past generations can be perceived in the well-worn sandstone floor and a hearth that has changed shape to accommodate the technological advances reflected in the Victorian range.

CORNWALL

$\mathscr{D}$OMINATING the sitting room of a small former miner's cottage are a Cornish range and several pieces of furniture that convey a sense of solidity that is in keeping with the area's granite surroundings and with the house's own construction.

DURHAM

*C*OMPLETELY rebuilt and furnished with total authenticity, the kitchen of this seventeenth-century farmhouse has a large fireplace that would have been used to spit-roast meat in front of the open flame. It was later fitted with a range, probably in the mid-nineteenth century. The room is adorned with a number of furnishings that recall the period.

SURREY

*I*N many cottages the space under the roof provides a vital area for storage. In this attic, however, the structure remains unaltered, and a living space has been inserted within it — even if the odd placement of the beams makes moving around slightly difficult.

SURREY

*T*HERE is a beauty in the sparse utilitarianism of this wash-house, exemplified by the sink made of a single piece of stone. Not only serving the needs of washing, the room also has a simple oven (left).

GLOUCESTERSHIRE

A TYPICAL feature of cottages in this area is the use of local limestone, which can be easily carved for lively decoration. In this cottage, such ornamentation – which is based on a medieval design – lends a touch of whimsy to the gravitas of the stone.

CORNWALL

*F*ILLED with books, pictures and a small
bed, the space of this tiny bedroom has been
used to the full by today's inhabitants. Some-
how, though, there is the feeling that it has
always looked this way.

CUMBRIA

*S*OME cottages, no matter how small, can be as elegant as the finest manor house. The dark wood of this cottage gives the sitting room a degree of distinction, while the built-in drawers flanking the fireplace make use of every inch of the limited living space.

OXFORDSHIRE

*T*HE tile-floored kitchen of this seventeenth-century workman's cottage is filled with interesting antiques and objects. The 1680 dresser and the shelves are built of English oak. The rows of bottles and jars, as well as the blue-and-white dinner service, contribute to the homely appeal of the room.

HAMPSHIRE

*T*HIS book-lined room was once used as a studio by the poet Edward Thomas, who lived nearby. It offered him a place to think and create, and today, with its mesmerizing shelves of books, the room is perfect for peaceful meditation.

GLOUCESTERSHIRE

*C*OTSWOLD limestone imparts warmth and solidity in this seventeenth-century miller's house, located in a valley near Stroud. The passage of time is noticeable in the nooks and crannies that have been worn into the soft stone over the years.

NORFOLK

———— ◆ ————

*A*N assortment of modest chairs surround a
table in the simply furnished living room
of a dairy cottage. To make the fireplace more
useful for today's needs, there is a brick box
that intensifies the fire within a small area.

———— ◆•◆ ————

CORNWALL

ON the Lizard Peninsula, inside a white-washed fisherman's cottage – a common sight in Cornwall – there is a comforting glow, a welcome retreat from harsh and unpredictable weather. Many of these cottages are huddled together on steep hills above the harbours.

ACKNOWLEDGEMENTS

Copyright © George Weidenfeld and Nicolson 1994

First published in Great Britain in 1994 by George Weidenfeld and Nicolson Ltd
Orion House, 5 Upper St Martin's Lane, London WC2H 9EA

British Library Cataloguing-in-Publication Data
A catalogue record for this book is available from the British Library

Cover and series design by Peter Bridgewater/Bridgewater Book Company
Series Editor: Lucas Dietrich

*Some of the material in this book was drawn from, among other sources, the Country Series
volume* English Cottage Interiors *by Hugh Lander and Peter Rauter.*